The Money Code
and
How to Crack It!

Everyday Lessons to Master the Mindset, Making, Maintenance and Multiplying Of Money

~

A book by: Stephanie J. Alvarez, Tesa Colvin, Sami Hageman, Gemma James, Dominique Mullally, Marnita Oppermann, Nicole Redmond & Maria Kathlyn Tan

Foreword by: Auguste Crenshaw, Business Coach, #1 Advanced Mental Conditioning Specialist for Entrepreneurs & Founder of the 'Real Women Don't Bitch Podcast'

The Money Code and How to Crack It!
Everyday Lessons to Master the Mindset, Making, Maintenance and Multiplying of Money

Authors:
Stephanie J. Alvarez – The Money Healer
Tesa Colvin – Business & Publishing Consultant
Sami Hageman – Accountant, MBA & Budgeting Boss
Gemma James – Advanced Law of Attraction & Wealth Practitioner
Dominique Mullally – Money & Mindset Coach
Marnita Oppermann – Mindful Money Coach
Nicole Redmond – Holistic Life & Business Coach
Maria Kathlyn Tan – Transformation Catalyst

All Rights Reserved
Published by Summit House Books (A Division of Borrow my MBA, LLC)
Cover Design by Lauria | eBook Cover Designs & Tesa Colvin
Money on White Background Photo Courtesy of Alexstar | depositphotos.com
Original Illustrations by Chelsea Patterson
Other charts/graphs by author(s)

ISBN-13: 978-1981328307
ISBN-10: 1981328300

References:
Discover Your Love Language, http://www.5lovelanguages.com/
Center for Poverty Research, University of California, Davis www.poverty.ucdavis.edu
The Bible, The New International Version (NIV)
Wi Xin Elements Graphic, https://en.wikipedia.org/wiki/Wu_Xing

DEDICATION

~ This book is dedicated to every reader who is ready to change their money lives. You are enough, and you deserve the peace, hope and joy around money that you dream of!

Abundance is your new normal. ~

TABLE OF CONTENTS

ACKNOWLEDGEMENT

Life is about learning. Were it not for the willingness of each of these authors to take their life lessons and use them to support others, this book would have never been have been possible.

Dominique, Nicole, Marnita, Maria, Gemma, Sami, and Stephanie, I wish each of you amazing women a consistent flow of blessings for your hard work on this project, as well as for your passion to serve others every single day. ~Tesa Colvin

4

FOREWORD

You already know that doesn't work and that is why certain topics cause you to shut down.

It is my firm professional standard, in order to help someone heal, neither party can conceal the hard facts. When a sensitive topic comes up my transparency is just as important as yours. I cannot speak to you from a place of theory. I reach you when I connect with you. Our belief is heightened when we see what is possible with regular people like us daily.

Get ready to go on a journey. See your life through the eyes of some amazing women who were just like you. Learn from their experiences and expert advice. No fluff, no bull. None of this six steps and you are done. See how you can take a deep dive but in a simple way to resolve your money issues. Not only are you going to address the issues from a practical perspective, get ready to dig into mindset and spirit. It is all connected.

In the entrepreneurial arena money is at the core of most issues. When your mindset and handling of money is off it can have the following impact.

You may price your products to low out of desperation. This will cause you to create a job you end up hating. This transcends into hating your dream.

You may price your products higher than your belief will allow and keep you from effectively selling. As a last result I have seen women give up on their dream.

You may desire to invest yourself, but the money magically disappears on a random expense when you need to move forward the most. This may cause you to question if you made the right decision to pursue your dream.

All of the above are unacceptable, but I see it in the industry every day. To save face many of these women say they need a self-care sabbatical or a moment away to revamp their business. They come back after exhausting the few funds they had to rebrand, only to end up doing it all over again or giving up. When the only thing they needed to do is get to the root of the issue.

This book is going to do that for you. These women are getting to the root.

The transparency is refreshing and will revive your hope.

Tesa Colvin spearheaded this "Movement" and that alone is enough for me to be excited. After multiple collaborative experiences, I can attest to the fact she walks the walk and stands in truth. This was truly a labor of love. She has a desire for you and your right to live life according to your terms.

While we all have similar experiences, there are foundational tools we all need, how we receive them varies. The individual issues vary. For that reason, Tesa knew she couldn't do this alone. She called out for the best and most compassionate women in the industry to keep it real with you.

It is time for your evolution.

If money talks and bullshit walks…

…let's have that money talk.

~**Auguste Crenshaw**~
Business Coach, #1 Advanced Mental Conditioning Specialist for Entrepreneurs & Founder of the 'Real Women Don't Bitch Podcast'

INTRODUCTION

When *The Money Movement Project* first crossed my mind I had no idea what the end result would look like or who would be involved. But I knew that there was a need for real conversations about the myths and miracles around money. And I knew that the time for those conversations was NOW!

So I went to work on finding the right super powers to help identify the root of some of the most common money experiences that people, specifically women, face. Working from a list of over 200 money experts of varying specialties, I reached out to person after person with one goal in mind. To have real conversations about their money stories, their methods, and their heart for their work.

Sure, the simple thing would have been to just do a call for authors or money experts and take the first "however many" people who signed up...

But the movement was, and still is, so much bigger than that.

This project required that each author not only give the bare, stripped down details of their fails, trials and falls, but also provide real actionable lessons that others could use to get results.

And of the hundreds of money specialist I connected with, there were 7 who stood out and stepped up to the challenge in a major way.

We've all come together to write a REAL, no fluff, and no B.S. book on money. From spiritual, to practical, we're talking about it.

Everyone has a money story, so as you read ours, get ready to take yours to a new level of amazing.

Chapter One
Changing Your Relationship with Money
~Marnita Oppermann~

We all have a money story. Your relationship with money starts the day that you are born, and will even outlive you, when your estate is finalized!

My own money story has led me to where I am today – where I can help others transform their stories too. Even with a degree in business, having studied accounting and working at one of the top accounting firms, in early 2015, I found myself drowning in debt, with no savings or future cushions to speak of. This resulted in even more debt after expenses and repayments, and this left me spinning in a vicious circle with nothing to live on.

I felt hopeless, anxious and desperate.

I had to do something.

I wanted a better life for myself – one of abundance, harmony and one where I could create a legacy, and not be a liability to those around me.

And so my money transformation journey began - with a single decision that I could no longer wait for someone to come and rescue me from my situation.

I had to armor up and save myself.

On my journey, I quickly discovered this profound truth:
My financial troubles had nothing to do with my accounting and math abilities and everything to do with my lack of a healthy relationship with money. A relationship that started in childhood, and led to me mirroring my parents' behaviour and language around money. But they were not at fault – of course they were not taught how to master their personal finances either.

I learned to identify the origins of my thought patterns which led me to change my behaviour towards money. My self-worth, beliefs and behaviours all contributed to my attitude towards my financial situation.
It was eye-opening and life-altering!

Through this journey, I not only transformed my relationship with money, I also managed to lose over 90lbs. A true body - mind - spirit transformation.

Today, my consumer debt has been paid off, money is flowing into my life in abundance and I have a financial freedom plan to secure my future. But most profoundly, I got clear on the vision for my life! I realised that my purpose is to help people who are ready to make the change and reach their full potential, through money coaching.

Maybe until now your relationship with money, like mine, has been rocky and a bit of a rollercoaster ride. Maybe you and money have even been on the brink of divorce! You desperately want to change your situation, but you do not know where to start.

I'd like to share the steps I took to help you get started:

Step 1: Make a decision to change

They say that the first step to change is the awareness that something isn't working in your life, and admitting your desire to make a change. By reading this book, you've already taken a giant leap to change your money story!

Step 2: Nurture your relationship with money

The second step is to work on your relationship with money including your mindset. Just like any ideal relationship, our relationship with money should be one of mutual respect and understanding. Money is a form of energy. You can either attract it, or push it away – whether consciously or subconsciously.

I invite you to start seeing money in a different light. To see money as a partner and friend who wants to support your every need and desire.

I regularly refer to 'The 5 Love Languages' by Gary Chapman. I use the Love Languages not only to improve my own personal relationships but also when I coach clients. It's an amazing relationship tool, not just for romantic relationships, but for friendships too.

The 5 Love Languages are:
Words of Affirmation
Acts of Service
Quality Time
Receiving Gifts
Physical Touch

I have two main Love Languages - Words of Affirmation and Physical Touch.

My love bucket is instantly filled when someone speaks these languages to me. They light up my soul! You can brighten my day by giving me a sincere big hug or telling me that you appreciate me or that I've made a difference in your life.

When two people's love languages are not a match, and they are not aware of this, it can cause friction in their relationship.

So what do the Love Languages have to do with money?

Whilst working on my relationship with money, I had a sudden realization. That money speaks in love languages too!

Money wants to **receive** Love through:

Using Words of Affirmation:

Money feels welcomed, appreciated and valued when you show it gratitude and respect, through your thoughts and words. If you are constantly criticizing money by speaking in a manner of lack, scarcity and fear, anger and frustration, money doesn't feel valued nor appreciated.

Who wants to stay in a relationship with someone who is constantly speaking negatively to and about them? You'd be out the door!

Remember that money is energy. It can feel the vibration you give out through your words and thoughts. You either attract through positivity or repel through negativity.

How can you turn a sour relationship around and show money your appreciation instead?

· **Gratitude**!
Instead of saying 'I'm broke', or 'I can't afford this', 'Say, WOW I have so much already!' and truly appreciate every single thing that money provides you with. Things like a home to be your sanctuary, food to nourish you, gas so that you can go places you need to be. Express your gratitude daily.
Think it. Speak it. Write it down.

Instead of using words which speak of a scarcity mindset, you could also say: 'My money has other priorities right now.' Just this subtle change of words, will shift your scarcity mindset. You are choosing to spend your money on what is priority at that moment. It's not a 'can't have' forever, just a 'no' for now.

· **Celebrate Money Magic**!
Don't you love it when someone is always excited to see you? Money loves that too! The law of attraction is simple - what you focus on, you'll get more of. If you focus on scarcity and lack, what

you'll get is more scarcity and lack. If you focus on abundance, you will attract even more abundance!

Words of Affirmation Homework:
- Get a Money Magic diary – any empty notebook that you can carry around in your bag will do.
- At the end of each day, write down three things you are grateful for and state WHY you are grateful for it. Your gratitude doesn't necessarily need to be money related – it can be for anything that made you feel wealthy and abundant that day.

    Here's an example: I am grateful for the friends I have, because they support, encourage, and bring me so much joy! In this sentence, I affirm the abundance of support, encouragement and joy I have in my life.

- Every time you pay a bill, buy your groceries or put gas in your car, consciously thank money for the value you are getting from the purchase.

- List any money magic that has happened during your day. Did you pick up a coin? Did a friend offer to buy your coffee? Did the taxman give you a refund? Did a client pay you early? Did you perhaps get a raise? Write it down! Celebrate money magic, big or small, and you'll notice more and more of it!

- Be mindful of the words you use when speaking about money. If you notice that you are speaking in a negative or limiting way, stop yourself and think of how you can change the statement into a more positive one.

Spending Quality Time:

Money loves spending time with you! Are you giving money the time and attention that it needs? When you have a 'head in the sand' approach when it comes to your finances or show ignorance and lack of care, can you blame Money for leaving you as quick as possible?

The old me, used to never want to look at my bank balance. At the till at the grocery store, when my phone beeped with the transaction message, I quickly made it disappear so I wouldn't see what my bank balance was. I just kept spending and hoped that it wouldn't run out. (Oh dear!)

Here's some of the ways you can practically use this language with Money:

· **Have regular money dates!**
Yes dates! When you sit with your budget (or as I'd like to call it, your 'Abundance Spending plan'), you are having a date. Make it light and fun – light a candle and make your favorite meal.

When you go through your expenses to make sure there aren't any areas of waste, you are spending quality time with money. When you work on your debt reduction plan, you are spending time with money. When you write in your Money Magic diary, you are spending time with money. It all adds up.

· **Get to know money through educating yourself!** When you read up on money and good money management, you are spending quality time with money. You can do this through subscribing to money blogs, joining money coaching webinars and reading books. There are many free ways in which you can get knowledge about money and empower yourself.

Or perhaps by meeting with your bank manager, a financial advisor or a money coach to help you get clarity and direction with your Money.

There is so much to know about money! It's a fascinating subject. Learn how it works, how to make it grow and flourish, how to get more of it, how to make it work for you.

By reading this book, you are showing your commitment to money and improving your relationship too!

In return, Money wants to show you so much love! Money does this through:

Acts of Service:

Money wants to serve and support you! Money wants to be there to help you live a prosperous abundant life. And enable you to live up to your full potential. Invite money to fulfil this role in your life!

Giving Gifts:

An abundance of gifts! Gifts to cover all your needs. Gifts of travel, gifts of amazing experiences, gifts of all your heart's desires. Accept the gifts that money wants to give you. The more you are supported and looked after, the more you are able to bless those around you with abundance too.

But like with any relationship that is going through strain, they say that the emotionally intelligent thing to do is, to swallow your pride and take the first step to repair the relationship.

It starts with YOU!

Start showing money love and care by using its love languages - and then see the magic unfold!

Declare to money that you are ready for a new journey, that you ask forgiveness for the neglect and abuse in the past and that you are committed to walk a new beautiful journey together.

Step 3: Take control of your finances

The third step in transforming your money story is to start taking control of your finances by doing the practical work.

I often get my inspiration from nature and use nature as a reference to explain the elements of financial wellbeing in my workshops and coaching.

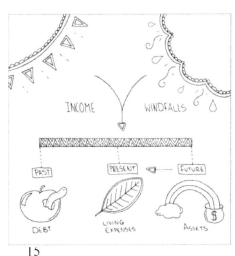

The illustration shows the flow of money into and out of your life:

Live well in the present
Clear the past
Prepare for the future

When money flows into your life, you can direct it to flow to one or more of these three categories – past, present and future.
Live well in the present:

'Creating financial freedom, has nothing to do with the amount of money that comes into your life, but what you do, with what you receive!'

How are you stewarding the money that comes into your life? Are you spending every last penny and then some more? Are you perhaps drowning in debt with no savings to show?

It's time to get clarity and take control of your monthly expenditure:

1. List all your fixed monthly bills (such as rent, insurances, utilities) and then your discretionary spending (e.g. food, entertainment, personal).
    Give your budget a spring cleaning. Perhaps it is cluttered with unnecessary expenses? Prioritise what is important to you. Eliminate waste and spending on things that no longer add value to your life.

2. Create a buffer – if you only apply one practical habit in your life after reading this, this should be it! This is your peace of mind fund - especially when paying off debt! Build a buffer of at least one month's worth of living expenses. Put this buffer in a separate account. Whenever money comes into your life (via a salary, or a windfall, or through any other income stream), allocate an amount towards your buffer BEFORE spending it on anything else! Yes, save before you spend. The initial amount does not matter, what is important is that you create the habit of saving. You are creating your

own safety net by doing this. When unexpected events occur, you can be your own bank and line of credit, and not resort to further debt! This money is only to be used for occasional events and not for every day expenses. This is absolutely key in breaking the spiral of debt.

Clearing the past:

'Bad debt is sacrificing your future day needs for your present day desires' –Suze Orman

Debt can wreck relationships, affect one's mental and physical health and ultimately destroy lives. This does not have to be your story! It doesn't matter what situation you find yourself in at this moment, there is a way out! Seek help if you need to – support goes a long way!

- Make a list of your debt, the interest rates and minimum payment amounts.
- Start by paying extra towards your smallest debt (emotional wins!). Once an account is paid up, add the amount you were used to paying, to the next creditor's payment. This way you not only pay your debt off faster, but you will also save on interest.
- Stop using more credit. Cut up your credit cards, close your accounts. Make a commitment to living a debt free life.
- Forgiveness is important when dealing with debt. The past is over. Mistakes have been made. Debt does not need to be a life sentence. It's time to let the past go and take daily steps towards a brighter debt free future!

Prepare for the future:

'If you don't find a way to make money while you're asleep, you will work until you die' – Warren Buffet

Are you preparing for the future? They say the best time to start saving for your financial freedom (when you no longer need to work for money) is the day you draw your first pay check. The next best time to start saving is now. As in right now, today.

Understandably, if debt is still a major factor in your life, your savings and investments will be on a smaller scale – in the interim. The key is to start, no matter how small. Even if you start by educating yourself on different investment and retirement options, and start putting a plan in place. As you eliminate debt from your life, you will be able to allocate more and more towards your future. This is where money thrives! And this is where the money that you've worked for will start working for you instead!

A healthy financial freedom plan may include the following:
- A cash based buffer of 3 – 6 months' worth of living expenses
- Retirement funds (country dependent)
- Tax Free Investment funds (country dependent)
- Unit trusts / stock market investments
- Other passive income streams

Take the time to educate yourself on all the different options and start implementing your financial freedom plan, step by step.

When money becomes a partner in your life instead of a slave driver, you will discover a harmony that you didn't even know existed before!

A few key things to remember:

Nurturing your finances:

- Is a balancing act between your relationship with money and practical healthy financial habits
- Is a process which takes dedication, determination and constant attention
- Is a form of self-care and self-love

- Can empower you in ways you could never imagine
- Will help you regain your confidence and help guide you to a prosperous future

You are worth it!

To find out what your Money Archetype is, check out the Money Quiz on my website: www.marnita.co.za/moneyquiz

Marnita Oppermann is a Mindful Money Coach and hails from Cape Town in South Africa. She combines her qualification and background in accounting, with her training as a Certified Money Coach (A qualification from The Money Coaching Institute in California).

She knows first-hand, that what seems daunting and overwhelming when attempted alone, is possible when we get guidance. We all need a sounding board, someone to listen and who cares to help us understand our thoughts, beliefs and behaviours and assist us to finally **do** the things we want to do rather than just talk about them.

She facilitates money mindset workshops, hosts online money courses, as well as work with individual clients, both locally and internationally. Her intention is to invite clients to experience the incredible, transformative impact changing their relationship with money can have on every aspect of their lives!

Her gift to you as reader: a 20 minute money coaching consult call. To claim this gift, contact her: info@marnita.co.za with 'The Money Code' in the subject line.

Facebook: https://web.facebook.com/marnitaoppermann/
Website: www.marnita.co.za

Chapter Two
Financial Trauma Momma
~Tesa Colvin~

My intention was to sit down and tell you how my financial trauma started 20 years ago, when my debit card declined, and the beautiful revelation that I had about simply knowing what's in your bank account.

But…

Within the past few days I realized that my trauma was even deeper than that.

I'm not gonna pretend that my relationship with money is perfect and uneventful. In fact, just as with any other relationship it takes work.

Not just sporadic work - but consistent, purposeful work.

Even as I write this, the impact of "consistency" is like a quick one-two punch for me.

To be honest my money story started without me even knowing it. I was a pregnant, 18 year old, working at a bank for $5.25 an hour, and my "had no" list was far longer than my "had" list.

- I had no driver's license
- I had no car

- I had no home of my own
- I had no education past a high school diploma
- I had no model in my life that showed me how to budget, save, **OR** manage credit

And worst of all I had no idea how these things were affecting me.

I struggled with so many things all rolled up into a neat package called my life. I was a pregnant black teen with no skills or education. I lived in a low income area that seemed to have been forgotten by all layers of government. And the religious background that I had, sentenced me to feeling like I deserved it because I was a sinning unwed mother.

So there I was not living, barely surviving, and feeling that I deserved every minute of it.

And that was only the beginning.

As time went on, I pushed those feelings of inadequacy down and took on the familiar mantra that "I was doing what I had to do for me and my baby."

But life was hard.

I felt alone, I felt valueless, and I felt like a burden and a blemish on society.

Why?

Because I needed help.
My family was not in a place to help me financially, the jobs I qualified for did one of 2 things:

Paid only some of the bills I had acquired.

Or

Changed my financial status making me ineligible for any type of government or social services and assistance.

I was in a dark, fruitless place filled with shoplifting for meals, writing bad checks to feed the now 2 children I had, having utilities shut off, cars repossessed, evictions (yes more than one), medical bills, lawsuits from creditors, threats of wage garnishments, multiple bankruptcies, and the list goes on and on.

The clear theme I carried around with me for many years was lack, because that is what I had evidence of.

The lack of money had showed up several times in my life in traumatic ways. It was consistent, relentless even.

And even when things seemed to be shifting in the right direction, there was the constant murmur inside my head that if I wasn't careful, lack would be around the next turn waiting to destroy all I'd worked for.

And you know what would happen?

I would be right!

Lack would pop-up in my finances, in my mindset, and even in my business.

I would worry about not having enough money to meet my family's needs, I would worry about how missing a payment or two or three would affect my credit, I would worry about not being able to pay bills, until I manifested those very things.

It's called self-fulfilling prophecy.

So you see even though I was no longer the pregnant teen, I had education, made $25 plus dollars an hour and then had my own business; I had not changed the most important aspect of my life.

It wasn't the external situations.

It was all those feelings, emotions and FEARS that I kept neatly packed inside my mind, spirit and soul.

Whatever level I moved to, they were there and would show up with a vengeance.

Even when I bounced back and got things back on track, the fear, anxiety and worry was there wreaking havoc.

So what do you do, when you have gone above and beyond to make sure that you will struggle and fail financially?

You have to take the time to be real with where you are in every aspect.

I started digging.

I wanted to be filled with peace, hope and joy when it came to my finances, right?

I didn't want to live paycheck, to paycheck.

I didn't want to be dead in the water whenever I had an emergency that required money.

I wanted to be a good steward and live in abundance...didn't I?

And the last question was where I struck gold. It was at that moment that the tears started flowing like rivers.

The phrase "good steward" took me back to my religious upbringing and the intense condemnation lessons that I was always taught.

The layers began to shed as I realized I didn't want to be abundant because I didn't think I qualified for it.

My life was a constant stream of not doing what the "theys" of the world thought, felt, or believed I should.

My take on my value and ability to generate income **AND** properly handle any income I got was falling between the cracks of my mindset and spirit at all times – without fail.

If I wanted things to change, I needed to face the problem head on. And that's when I realized that I'd spent years confusing "being a good steward" with a deep rooted and extreme fear of lack.

I needed a game plan, one for every aspect of my money life.

So I went to work.

The first step was Mindset.

The trauma of lack had resulted in an unhealthy mindset and perspective on my value and it manifested in my money.

I needed immediate reprograming! This was a 2 fold process including affirmations and scriptures.

For the affirmations piece, I made sure I not only wrote strong affirmations about myself, my worth and my money, but I took it a step further and recorded myself reading them. This was powerful because it resulted in me hearing positive- life giving words ABOUT me and money, in my own voice.

The second part of the plan came from a conversation with a close friend of mine, who is a premier mindset specialist. And she suggested that I take a look at those religious condemnations that I had internalized, and make a list of scriptures that say otherwise.

So I replaced "I am less than because I was a single mother" with "I am fearfully and wonderfully made".

"I've made mistakes, so I deserve to struggle" was replaced with "I am the head and not the tail, above ONLY and not beneath",

I did this for EVERY SINGLE one of those negative thoughts.

And the beautiful part is that this list is a living list – meaning that I can continue to add to it.

Why is that important?

Because for every new level you graduate to, improving your money mindset or mindset period will uncover new thoughts and limitations that need to be addressed.

I found that fear had taken up residency in my mindset and affected every aspect of my life and money life.

And when there's a massive trickle down affect like what I faced, there is a need to expand the plan of attack.

Let's do the work:

1) **Don't just scratch the surface of your mindset work.** Really dig in and examine your senses around your money mindset. What is the look, feel, taste, smell of your response to money in your life?
   o Remember, on the surface I believed that I truly wanted abundance, when the reality was I wanted abundance to combat lack. That energy was out of alignment with the manifestation of Abundance.
   o Ask yourself the deep questions like:
      i. Who deserves money?
      ii. How do you feel about people with money?
      iii. Do you think you're supposed to give money away?
      iv. Do you think that it's unfair when other people have money?

2) **Look at your mindset from specific angles.** Look at it specific to money making, money maintenance, and even the multiplying of money.
   o For example, when I looked at my mindset specific to making money, I realized that I struggled in that area because of an issue I had with valuing myself. Still a mindset issue, but the root is not fear alone.

- For instance when you do this, what are your rules about making money?
  i. Should it be hard to make money?
  ii. Should it be easy to make money?
  iii. Do some people have an unfair advantage?
  iv. What is your process or approach to money maintenance?
  v. Do you feel like it's too complicated to maintain money?
  vi. Do you feel that financially successful people have access to resources that you don't?
  vii. How simplistic is it to really maintain and manage your money?
  viii. Why do you think like this?
  ix. Are you not embracing doing money maintenance because you're embarrassed to get help (i.e. an accountant, group or budgeting class)?

3) **Don't just make note that there is a mindset issue, incorporate actions that will help you improve your mindset as well as new limitations you discover.** This is necessary because each layer or level will expose a new area you need to work to improve.
   - An example of this is my "living affirmation list". Not only does it speak to beliefs that I have stamped out, it helps me address more as I graduate.
   - Also, a physical action would be to make sure that you KNOW your finances. Not obsess or worry about, but clearly note monthly bills, their due dates, when they're late, what's set up on automatic withdrawal. You will also want to note income that you have coming in. Don't over think this. A notepad, calendar, or spreadsheet will do the trick. See the example below:

Bill	Amount	Due Date	Late Date	Jan (10)
Mortgage	800	1st	15th	X
Auto Insurane	132.15	1st	N/A	X
Gym	54.95	1st	N/A	X
Student Loans	85	6th	N/A	X
Power	226	8th	9th	X
Car Payment 2	453.31	14th	15th	X
Water	89	15th	16th	X
Car Payment 1	458.44	15th	N/A	X
Cell Phone	289.94	16th	17th	X
Phone/Internet	116	16th	25th	X
Alagasco	60	26th	N/A	X
Hulu	7.99	29th	N/A	X
Netflix	9.99	30th	N/A	X
Trash Pick Up	39.97	Quarterly	N/A	N/A
*Autodrafts				

Income	Amount	Due Date	Method
Husbands Pay	1500	1st	Auto Deposit
Client 1	500	1st	Auto Deposit
Client 2	250	1st & 15th	Auto Deposit

4) **Mindset trauma requires the same dedication and consistency as a physical trauma.** Journaling one time, or saying an affirmation one time will allow you to check things off your "to-do" list, but it will not help you to truly change things.
- o Think about an athlete who gets hurt. They don't just get a diagnosis and treatment; they also get physical therapy to make sure that they come back stronger than before. The same is true of mindset. You don't want to just "get-over" the issue you had, you want to strengthen your mindset for the future.
- o To be sure that you are consistently working to turn things around, here is a 21 day plan to help you get clear on your mindset state AND where you are financially.
    - i. **Week 1** – Journal as much as you can about money to make sure you truly embrace your issue with your money mindset. Write out every single time something (thought or emotions) comes up for you around money.

For example if you get a feeling of dread when you go to the gas station because you are spending money "again" and you can't buy yourself something you want or need.

  ii. **Week 2** – Journal as much as you can around making money whether in your job or business. When you have thoughts of anxiety, jealousy of others perceived financial status, stress, take a moment and really journal out and get to the root of it.

  iii. **Week 3** – Journal all of your brainstorming, epiphanies from previous journaling, and your work getting clear on what's coming in and going out as far as your finances.

Improving my mindset habits, led to better, wiser actions from the beginning, and not just in an effort to repair problems after the fact.

So if you're reading this, and you feel like you're in a financial situation so dire that you should skip past the mindset work, I can honestly tell you that is not the case.

You need mindset to get out of the bed in the morning.

Look back at my story, even when my financial situation changed, I did not have the right mindset to maintain where I was or move to a higher level.

If you're tired of being stuck in a hellish repeat of the same situations, it's time to check the constant…you and your thought life.

Once you get your mindset muscle up, you will also gain clarity on the proper actions to take to improve the different facets of your money life.

Tesa Colvin is the Owner and CEO of Borrow my MBA, LLC, a Bestselling Author, Business & Publishing Consultant. She helps Service Based Business Owners like Coaches, Consultants & Speakers write well positioned books focused on their expertise that can be leveraged to get more clients, speaking engagements and opportunities for their businesses.

She uses her MBA, and 8+ years of combined business coaching and publishing experience to offer tailored support and guidance to help entrepreneurs not just set goals, but develop effective plans that help them to reach their financial goals with their branded business books.

And when she's not helping people find success their way, you can find her tucked away in a quiet space creating words, worlds and characters, or having a Michael Jackson sing off with both her daughters while her husband and 2 fur babies watch in horror.

To stay connected feel free to reach out to her directly at info@borrowmymba.com!
Facebook: https://www.facebook.com/BMyMBA/
Website: http://borrowmymba.com/

Chapter Three
Money, Your Spirit Partner: Why Loving Money Honors Spirit
~Maria Kathlyn Tan~

I was born and raised in the Philippines, a country predominantly Catholic.

Like most entrepreneurial Filipino-Chinese families, mine paid homage to both Catholic Churches and Buddhist temples.

We paid tribute to different saints and different gods. Some of the members in my family took *"panata"* or *"vows/oath"* of paying homage to certain churches and temples on certain days. There were "Divine helpers" to call on for specific reasons like:

> *St. Jude for miracles and hope*
> *Sto. Niño (Child Jesus) for innocence, miracles, protection and family*
> *Guan Yin for mercy and compassion*
> *Tsai Shen Yeh for prosperity and protection*

I've always had a lot of "Spirit Beings" to call on whenever I am stuck or whenever things weren't going my way.

In my mid-twenties, though, I went through an unprecedented phase of depression. My life felt so empty, and I couldn't make sense of my existence.

I was making relatively good money for my age. I had become financially independent from my family. I didn't have children. I was not in a serious relationship and I wasn't in a hurry to have one.

In short, **nothing was tying me down.** The only person I was responsible for was me.

Yet my disposable income and "free" lifestyle wasn't filling the void that kept growing in my chest.

I didn't feel relevant, and even imagined being dead and no one really noticing.

During this time I grew to hate money. My life until then was focused on the pursuit of a 'successful' life measured by this checklist that was a consensus in the environment I grew up in:

- Get good grades
- Graduate
- Work experience (get a good job or start a business)
- Gain independence
- Make money

By age 25, I had so much work experience in different fields that nothing excited me.

I worked in the private and public sector.

I did some freelancing.

I was consulting.

I was teaching.

I was writing.

As I took on project after project the *money poured in*. The increasing bank balance was more than welcomed **until I started resenting it.** It became a symbol of life slowly disappearing in front of me. I saw where I was probably headed: *a young, jaded, cynical* *millennial who felt life cheated her of something and whose life had become black and white, devoid of any color.*

For a while I played victim and blamed money.

> *I had money. I could buy whatever I wanted. But nothing I bought thrilled me. I wasn't happy. Why wasn't I happy?*

Things weren't adding up. I kept seeing money as the villain. Thoughts like, *"Because of money, I didn't pursue what I loved and what I should be doing."* kept circling in my head.

I was stuck at the thought that I wasn't living my purpose because I was doing things purely for money.

I began viewing money as the **anti-Spirit / anti-God**. I started believing *doing things for money was evil*. Purpose should be the sole focus. I have to find Purpose and then I can feel happy. I scoffed at money and everything that money gave me.

For a few years, I went on a deep pursuit of *"spirituality"* - *the quest to be aligned with my soul and the Spirit.* I yearned to understand what I was here for. I was hungry to make a difference.

I took on work that I thought filled my soul but didn't bring me much money.

Every time I felt like I was being taken advantage of, I told myself, *"I'm not doing this for the money."*

I was so desperate to find my purpose and my desire to be happy was so strong that I ignored every instinct that told me to pause and take it all in. I just kept going and going until once again I shut down emotionally, mentally and 'spiritually'.

Again, there was something wrong with the picture. I was doing work that was supposed to fill my soul. I was doing everything I could to live according to God's (Spirit's) plan. I was no longer in the pursuit of the material.

So why was I feeling duped by life once more?

I started reading and studying about the different elements / natural components that make up this world - fire, earth, air and water. I compared what I knew of Chinese philosophy and why there is a fifth element that doesn't have a counterpart in what's widely-accepted in the West.

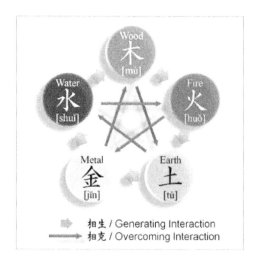

Huo = Fire
Tu = Earth
Jin = Air (Metal- metallic elements in the air)
Shui = Water
Wood = ?

I thought back to how people lived their lives in the past. Long before gods and goddesses and the different factions of religion, *humans worshipped nature* **to pay tribute to an all-encompassing Spirit.**

Even today, when we speak of nature, the first image that usually pops into our minds is the **woods.**

Following this thread of thought, I came to one conclusion:

What the Chinese philosophy takes as wood is simply Spirit

Thus -

At the crux / core of everything - of all the four elements or natural components of this world, Spirit is what ties everything together.

And so if I simplify things in life and use the same regenerative relationship that the Chinese, with their 5000 years of history, are using, then this is the basic pattern:

Spirit/God/Greater Power (Wood) gives us an impulse or a spark (Fire) to take action (Earth) and act on a new idea (Air/Metal). We have to effectively communicate (Water) this so as to invite the rest of the Universe (Spirit) to help us.

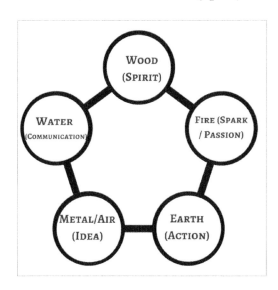

Therefore,

If my purpose is whatever was downloaded from Spirit, then the four other elements are in play.

I need Fire to keep my passion burning.

I must translate the passion to this Earth in the form of action.

I have to formulate my idea clearly and project an Air of clarity.

I should Water down so I can effectively communicate (or else my passion will get ahead of me)

...I need all of the four above *to have the rest of the World and all of the Universe (Spirit) help me in carrying out my purpose.*

So if it's as simple as this, why aren't many people living their purpose? One word:

MONEY

For anything to move in the world we live in, Money is involved one way or another. This is why we call money "currency".

For things to be current, movement needs to be present. For movement to happen, there are currents.

And if we term the cohesive streams of water moving in the ocean as currents, and circulation is simply currency, then Money is necessary.

For me to be in my purpose today, I need the rest of the Universe to receive and accept my ideas or thoughts. For that, I need to communicate effectively.

If I need to sometimes water down my thoughts and ideas so I can simplify things and make things more current and create movement, then a currency (Money) is necessary.

36

Therefore,

Money is at the crux of everything, right alongside Spirit.

And Money, when viewed not as "good" or "evil", but simply as what it is -

currency - presence - movement

All are imperative in living my purpose.

Once I simply accepted these facts, I shifted gears. *From resenting Money, viewing it as the anti-God or anti-Spirit and being the scapegoat to all my woes, I started re-casting Money from the villain to the supporting actor in the life story of which I'm the main character.*

I realized that casting money as my Spirit Partner made all these possible:

Comfort - I have a home that I love. I easily afford impulsive buys. I easily decide - I don't overly think on whether or not to buy something. I can afford "losing" money and not cry over spilled milk - in terms of bad financial investments.

Convenience - With Money as my Spirit Partner, I have easily afforded to think, "Convenience over costs". Unless I want the exercise, I take a cab somewhere. When I head home for a week, I stay at a hotel for 3 days because I can't easily work at home. If I want coffee but can't be bothered by making coffee, I head out and head to the nearest convenience store to get one. Seeing Money as a currency just freed me from debating too much on whether to buy or not to buy.

Connection - Money affords me many connections - friends, new ideas, new places to visit, new experiences. Money has allowed me to open myself up and connect more with people through being able to easily go out for coffee, lunches, dinners. Money has also made it possible for me to test my ideas, to experience new things, to engage in activities, to travel to different places.

Money helps me multiply my impact. It has made living my purpose much easier. With Money as my friend, I have one less thing to worry about.

If you haven't started viewing money as your Spirit Partner, you are robbing yourself of all the possible *currency - presence - movement* you need to live your purpose.

Start listing all the benefits that money has afforded you over the years. As you do this you will create a new relationship with your **Spirit Partner, Money.**

For you to reflect on:

What are the comforts money has given me? List at least 10.

_____

_____

_____

_____

_____

What are the conveniences that money has afforded me? List at least 10.

_____

_____

_____

_____

_____

What are the connections I've gained because of money? List at least 10.

_____

_____

_____

_____

_____

In what ways can Money help me today? List at least 7.

_____

_____

_____

_____

_____

In what ways can Money be my friend? List at least 7.

_____

_____

_____

_____

In what ways can Money be my Spirit Partner? List at least 7.

_____

_____

_____

_____

_____

How can I start treating Money with love? List at least 5.

_____

_____

_____

_____

_____

How can I start giving Money respect? List at least 5.

_____

_____

_____

_____

How can I honor Money? List at least 5.

_____
_____
_____
_____
_____

Why should I make money? List at least 3.

_____
_____
_____
_____
_____

Why should I love money? List at least 3.

_____
_____
_____
_____
_____

Why should I give and receive money? List at least 3.

_____
_____
_____
_____
_____

What is one thing I can do to incorporate money in my everyday life?

_____
_____
_____
_____
_____

"I look at Money as my Spirit Partner.
With Money I can fulfill my mission here on earth.
I need not worry about other things!"
- *Miracle Maria*

Maria Kathlyn Tan (aka Miracle Maria) is an expert in leveraging all of her experience. She strongly advocates radical self-acceptance and being in the *Business Of Me* as a means to having a fulfilled and joyous life.

She works with ambitious soul-centered individuals to fully capitalize on who they are and what they bring to the table. She flourishes when she's in a variety of activities and is active in different business and social groups, both local and international.

You can get a glimpse of how you monetize on you by taking her signature online quiz - http://maria-miracles.com/business-miracle-quiz/

Facebook: https://www.facebook.com/everylittlemiraclecounts/
Website: http://maria-miracles.com/

Chapter Four
We Didn't Know We Were Broke
~Sami Hageman~

There we were in our early thirties, a year and half into our young marriage and we were broke.

We didn't know we were broke though.

We were living comfortably, or so we thought. We weren't delinquent on any payments, we had food on the table, and we were able to go on trips and nights out with friends without even blinking. We were having fun and soaking up our new life together. From the outside looking in, we were doing great.

The conversation inside of our home told a different story. You see, I have an accounting degree and an MBA. I thought that I knew what I was doing with our money. We were budgeting every month and like I said, we weren't delinquent in any area. Sure, there were times in my college years where swiping my debit card at the store was a gamble. But that wasn't the problem here. The problem was the crushing amount of debt we had and the fact that we were making only minimum payments on it.

At the time, debt was normal to me.

It was something I assumed I would have for years. Maybe even forever. Debt is something everyone has, right? And I thought, there is "good debt" like mortgages, cars and student loans and there is "bad debt" like credit cards and home equity lines. I bought into the lie that debt is normal. I remember thinking that to myself and getting a gut check that I was wrong. But like many, I ignored it and continued on with my debt filled life.

Enter the hero of the story, my husband, Dallas. He, on the other hand, didn't agree with me. He would say things like "We make way too much money to be this far in debt." He continued to question my mindset and encourage the idea that we *could* actually pay off all of our debt. It took me a while to come around but eventually I agreed and we got to work.

At the end of 2015 we sat down and made some goals for the following year. We made an aggressive goal to pay off $40k in debt in 2016. I didn't think it was possible but we set the goal and I started budgeting. We more than doubled that debt payoff amount in 2016 and paid off over $88k that year.

Fast forward to July 2017, we paid off the last of our debt and can actually say that we are 100% debt free!

We started out in January 2016 owing a little more than $186k and by the time we made our last payment, we had paid off nearly $195k in 18 months. The delta there is the interest that accumulated while we paid off the debt. It goes without saying, that type of progress took a lot of hard work and dedication. It required us to sacrifice and make tough decisions. It also means that we changed the way we looked at debt and the way we looked at money. Our mindset with money shifted completely, it had to or we wouldn't have accomplished nearly what we did.

In an age where we have a constant stream of other people's success on our social media feeds, we had to learn not to compare our situation to others. The debt we had, consisted of a mortgage, student loan debt, a few credit cards and a vehicle loan. That combination of debt is not uncommon among households. We learned through this process though that the uncommon part is actually paying the debt off. We quickly realized that if we wanted to achieve our financial goals, we could no longer want the same lifestyle as our friends. You know the saying, "keeping up with the Joneses"? That had to stop. We learned that there was no way for us to achieve our version of financial success if we worried about what others were doing or what they thought of our financial situation.

We also had to learn that money is a tool. That it is a blessing and not a curse. And that we can use it to do great things. It took us accruing a lot of debt and then paying that debt off to realize that we weren't made to just work and pay bills. That we could actually work to live and not live to work because we owed so much. Our mindset shifted from making money to buy more stuff to making money to achieve goals. What a difference!

It absolutely amazes me to see how differently we approach purchases now. We walk into a store and see a lot of nice products to decorate our home with or use for different purposes. Our mindset has shifted in a way that we know how purchasing an item will impact our goals. We are now so intentional with our spending that accumulating a bunch of stuff has no appeal to us. Now, that's not to say that we don't spend money but we are just critical of each purchase. We appreciate how long it took us to earn that money and are cautious to spend it when not necessary.

I think the problem with money is that none of us were ever really taught how to handle it properly. With my education and background, you would think that I would be someone who would know how to handle my personal finances. But the truth is, I was never really taught how to budget or spend carefully. All I did was watch what others were doing and followed along.

That brings us to my first tip, do not just watch what others are doing and assume that's what you should do too.

If you're reading this book, you're on the right track. Find resources and other people who are winning with money and start learning from them. You'll likely find that they care less about how new their car is and more about how big their bank account is.

I mentioned earlier that the first step in our journey was to set some goals related to our finances. If you want to win with money you have to shift your mindset from spend, spend, spend to goal,

goal, goal. Take some time and think about what you really want to achieve with your money. Maybe you want to give like crazy or buy your dream home. Think big! Start with your five year goal(s), then determine what goal(s) you need to achieve in four, three, two and one year to help you achieve that big goal.

From this point on you'll focus all of your efforts on achieving that first year goal. Your mindset should shift from that next trip to the mall, to hitting your goal on time or maybe even sooner. Make sure your goals are clearly defined, can be measured in some way and are realistic. So, "I want to be a millionaire" doesn't work. It is not clearly defined, measured and depending on your circumstances, it may not be realistic. Something like, "I want to have a million dollar net worth within five years" meets the criteria. It is clearly defined that you want to have a million dollar net worth, it is measured within five years and if you're earning enough or have a decent start, it very well could be realistic.

To help you stay focused on your goals, post the most current goal somewhere in your home. We use a simple small chalk board and update our progress as we go. It's kept in our kitchen as a daily reminder of what we're working toward. We find that it is a great way to keep us both up to speed on our progress since I'm the primary budgeter. We also keep pictures on our phone of what our big goal is.

We can reference those anytime we have a weak moment or are struggling to stay on track.

Now that you have your goals set, it is time to start budgeting. Our budget was the number one tool we used to pay off all of our debt. We will actually be budgeting every month for the rest of our lives because having a plan with your money is the best offense. Our budget keeps us from wasting money, allows us to spend money on what's important to us and helps us achieve our goals. Budgets are often misconstrued as limiting but using a budget freed us from debt and gave us great hope.

We complete a zero based budget every month. This means that with each paycheck we zero our bank account. Full disclosure, we have a $50 buffer in our account just in case I make a mistake. I'm good but not perfect! This method of budgeting requires us to make a name, so to speak, for every dollar so that we cannot waste it on something else. It's easy for budgeting to sound overwhelming or complicated but that's simply not the case. All you have to do is jot down your monthly bills and paychecks in order of date. Take your paycheck amount and deduct each bill amount. If you have any left over after you've paid all of your bills, bought groceries and anything else you needed, you will put the rest of that money toward your goal. So if you're paying off debt, all of the extra will go to debt. If you're saving, boom, you just increased your savings account.

Paycheck	$1,500.00
Tithe	$ (155.00)
Auto Insurance	$ (85.00)
Life Insurance	$ (35.00)
Mortgage/ Rent	$ (700.00)
Electric	$ (75.00)
Grocery Week 1	$ (75.00)
Fuel Week 1	$ (40.00)
Entertainment Week 1	$ (25.00)
Trash	$ (20.00)
Grocery Week 2	$ (75.00)
Fuel Week 2	$ (40.00)
Entertainment Week 2	$ (25.00)
Savings	$ (150.00)

Here is an example of a zero based budget for one paycheck. If you add up all of the bills and deductions they will equal the full $1,500 paycheck. Bottom line, just set a budget. It doesn't have to be a zero based budget, it doesn't have to be in an app or in excel, just as long as you set one and stick to it you'll be moving in the right direction! Bonus: If you head to my website, you can snag my budget templates for free!

Once you've set your goals and your budget, the real work begins. You really have to change your view of money and how you spend it. Honestly, you have to get sick of your current situation. You have to get mad at the status quo. Only you can turn your finances around and you've got to motivate yourself to get it done! You also have to believe that you can accomplish great goals with your finances. Sure, we all won't be billionaires but we all can accomplish our own version of financial success. Will it take hard work and dedication? Absolutely! But I can tell you, it will be well worth it.

From this point forward, you no longer have to accept that debt is the answer. You do not have to take out a loan for a car. Save up some cash and buy a reasonable, reliable vehicle. Those credit cards in your wallet, cut them up!!! Instead of relying on credit cards for an emergency, set aside some funds that will be your bail out. We have six months' worth of expenses in our savings account and will never again rely on a credit card to get us through again. While we were paying off debt we had $1,000 in our savings account. Set an amount aside that works for you and your family. My point is, there are ways to navigate your finances without leaning on debt. You just have to break out of the mold and out of what society thinks is normal.

Believing in yourself and in the possibility of achieving your goals is critical to your success. Everything around you tells you that it is not possible. Someone will always have a nicer home or car. Someone will always have a bigger bank account. It is so easy to compare yourself to others and put yourself down. But you have to be your own biggest fan, get your surroundings out of your head, hunker down and focus on your own success.

I suggest finding someone who is winning with money and ask them to mentor you. Make sure this person is actually winning with money and not just pretending like the masses. This person can cheer you on and offer advice when you need it. They can also hold you accountable to your financial goals and speak into your life when you're slipping up. This relationship can help you keep your focus and help you achieve your goals.

You'll also have to start finding contentment in what you have. This step is critical. If you're just starting out, you'll likely cut expenses and really pair down what you spend your money on. Which, by the way, is exactly what you should do! You'll have to say 'no' to yourself and others a lot. Somedays are harder than others but this behavior is absolutely how you will win with money. This will require you to find contentment in what you have and what you're doing. You'll probably get creative to keep yourself entertained, it's not all that glamorous, but remember; this behavior now will pay off big later.

Some quick tips to get you started:

1. If you have a big auto loan or a larger home than you need, consider selling. Downgrade now so that you can accomplish your goals. You can always drive a really nice car later or buy that dream home when you pay cash or can afford it!

2. Since we're talking about selling, sell some unneeded stuff around your home! Use the proceeds to achieve your current goal quicker.

3. Get to work! Think about getting a second job or advancing your career. If you earn more and are budgeting wisely you'll see great success with some increased income coming your way!

4. Don't be stingy! I am all about frugality and spending wisely but one area we never slipped in was our giving. We tithe a full 10% of our gross earnings every month and encourage you to do the same. This is the only time in the bible where God tells you to challenge Him and from personal experience, His promise rings true! Not Christian? Still give 10% to an organization you have vetted and believe in. Giving will ensure that the way you're handling your money aligns with your beliefs and will give you a greater purpose to what you're achieving.

5. Cut your expenses. I talked about this earlier but if you're swimming in debt or have big goals to achieve, that cable TV may not look so appealing. Find cheaper options to cable,

eating out, clothes shopping and even your cell phone expense. You'll be shocked at what you can save!

6. Start paying with cash for groceries, clothes and entertainment. Really, use cash in any area you tend to over spend. You'll likely spend less with cash and will stay right in budget.

7. Don't be afraid to be different. I'm telling you right now, you will be different. We always say if folks look at us like we're crazy that means we're doing it right! Work hard and work toward what your version of success is!

You might be thinking to yourself, "Wow, this is all really easy for her to say!" But remember, my husband and I have been there, we destroyed a mountain of debt and now have great peace in what our finances look like. We know that you can do it too! I really do believe that winning with money is 90% mindset and 10% behavior. Having the right mindset, setting goals and a budget will certainly create a recipe for success. I also believe that anyone, and I mean anyone, can win with money.

Even you.

If you're looking for a sign to turn your financial life around, this is it! Now get to it!

Set your goals!!

Goal Setting Template
5 Year Goal
4 Year Goal
3 Year Goal
2 Year Goal
1 Year Goal
Make sure your goals are clearly defined, can be measured and are realistic.

Sami Hageman is the Owner of Eat Pray Budget, LLC, an accountant/MBA by day and a budgeting boss by night. She helps young couples, singles and families develop budgets and spending habits to win with their money. Her personal experience of paying off a substantial amount of debt with her husband lit a passion she didn't know existed. She uses her accounting background, MBA and real life experience to offer solutions to those struggling with achieving their financial goals.

When she's not helping people with their personal finances, she and her husband enjoy traveling and taking in any adventure that life throws at them. She loves a quite night in, an excellent meal at a local eatery and a good glass or wine!

To stay connected head over to Sami's website, www.eatpraybudget.com or reach out via email to info@eatpraybudget.com.

Chapter Five
Survivor's Mindset versus Abundance Mindset
~Nicole Redmond~

It was 30 minutes before work was over for the day. I had been thinking of 50 million little white lies to tell anyone with a sympathetic ear at Quickstart Payday Loans about why I was not able to make my bi-weekly installment payment. Simply stating I didn't have the funds, was not enough in my mind. I've been in situations like this before and most people understood financial hardships. I was the Queen of financial hardships. Though most of them were in my mind and behaviors at the time.

I had been out of the Army for almost a year. My husband, at the time, was deployed, and I was on my first civilian job getting paid $12.75/hr. We lived in a military town, Fort Hood, Texas. Fort Hood, was my last duty station before I received my honorable discharge on April 2, 2004. I was a Non-commissioned officer, a Sergeant, E-5 to be exact. When I arrived at Fort Hood, I had plans of becoming a Warrant Officer. However, things immediately changed when we arrived in February 2004 to the military base to sign into our units. We'd both just come from spending 15 months in Korea. My baby girl at the time was living with my mom in Tampa, Florida. The saying, "if you want to make God laugh, tell him your plans", was the premise of my situation. I had plans, but God had something else in mind.

Earning $12.75 an hour in Central Texas was decent pay for a civilian according to the average person living in the surrounding areas. My pockets and bank account said otherwise. I made less than

$30,000 a year as compared to making approximately $50,000 plus in the Army. An E-5 back then with over 6 years active duty pay was around $2,130.60 per pay period. Simply stated, I took one hell of a pay cut on the way out. To put the icing on the cake, I was not financially prepared to get out of the military. Healthcare, steady pay, and automatic PAID leave, were just some of the many perks the military offered compared to working as a civilian and having to earn it after so many days on the job, or worst, not at all. Worst of all, you don't get paid when you miss work.

I was just trying to survive and that was my mindset.

I immediately left work and drove to Quickstart Payday Loans with a great excuse in mind. When I got there, I waited in line patiently. Nonchalantly looking around but still on edge, hoping that no one would recognize me. The chime of the door opening kept me frantically alert. I was next in line. I sadly expressed to the woman behind the glass that I was short on my paycheck from being sick from work and needed an extension. *"Tell me lies, tell me sweet little lies"*, by Fleetwood Mac…played in my head. She kindly understood and proceeded to explain the additional fees that I would incur for extending the loan. I was granted some more time, but interest was the penalty for having survivor's mentally and a broke spirit.

The amount of money that I borrowed a month prior was $1,500. I owed them a total of $4,229.75. ***More than double what I borrowed!*** At the time, I didn't truly pay attention to what I was obligated to pay back when I went to the store and signed the loan agreements. I just knew I needed the money to keep the lights on. You'd think since my husband was in the military, we would be o.k. with finances. NOT! It was the complete opposite. He had a habit of taking advances on his check and leaving me with the rest to maintain the house we were renting at the time. Every pay period he would take about $300-$500 dollars out. I couldn't figure out for the life of me what the hell he was spending it on since he was in Iraq. It was a tough time, he was due to come home in a month and I honestly was enjoying my time away from him.

The next morning, I received an alert saying my account had an overdraft. I took a very deep breath and began my day. I prepared my daughter's lunch and put on her clothes. She didn't want for anything. If anyone in the house was going to suffer, it was going to be me. She was 3 years old at the time. The night prior we had a couple of cans of pork and beans with hot dogs from the dollar store because that was all I could afford.

I arrived to work around 7:30 a.m. I immediately called the automated line at my bank to check my account. The account was $564.25 overdraft. Quickstart Payday Loans had drafted funds from my account that I didn't have. Then tack on overdraft fees and pending transactions...I was screwed and felt sick to my stomach. On my breaks, I would look in the telephone book for other quick cash stores I had not been to, to see about getting another loan. I was living in a never-ending cycle of robbing Peter to pay Paul because I had a survivor's mentality when it came to finances and didn't know at the time that I had *self-inflicted financial trauma*.

The only reason I was in that predicament was that we didn't have enough to cover the bills and we didn't manage our finances effectively. I was literally putting myself through financial hell because I didn't understand and have the knowledge to be in a better position.

One month later...

I had dressed attractively in my eyes, even though my mind knew I had gained an extra 50 pounds. I prepared our daughter in the cutest outfit. We went on the military base to 1st Cavalry Division field to receive the soldiers that had arrived back from Iraq. Though I was not happy the husband was back, it was a relief to see his face. Our daughter was exceptionally happy to see her daddy. He gave her, our little girl, a huge hug and spun her around in the air. She smiled and giggled like any free-spirited child would. He looked at me with the *Grinch that stole Christmas* grin and said, "Got-dawg Aretha Franklin", pointing out my obvious weight gain. *What an ass!* He gave me a mediocre hug and we all loaded up in the SUV.

"Let's swing by the ATM," he requested with excitement.

Though I knew there was absolutely nothing to be excited about. He had less than $3,000 in his account. I managed to save that from blood, sweat, and ignorance. We pulled up to the ATM machine. He pushed in his pin code and proceeded through the prompts. The ATM machine spit out a receipt with the balance.

"What the hell is this? Where is my money?" he yelled.

"You spent it in Iraq. That is what is left," I replied.

"There should be way more money than this! What did you do with my money?"

"Are you kidding me? Your money? We have a house we are renting. A 3-year old. Daycare expenses, food expenses, expenses and more expenses. I am not in the Army anymore, remember!"

Our daughter began to cry in the backseat. As we continued to argue to the point that I zoned out.

The rest of the conversation was a series of Blah, BLAH, BLAH, money…blah, blah, blah, mine…blah, BLAH, blah, Blah, bullshit!

I believe that was the moment God planted the seed to manifest in me to do better. However, that was just the beginning of my journey. I'd endure several more years of mistakes and hardships before my breakthrough came.

Life is _your_ best teacher and can be _your_ worst enemy when you don't adhere to what the wind is saying when it blows…

The winds of life have taught me several things on this journey about having a survivor's mindset and living in a survival mode…

First, when in survival mode, **everything is in the moment and sporadically executed.** For us, at that time, there was no long-term planning, savings, and better future when it came to our finances.

Second, when in survival mode, **there was no control of our money. In fact, money was in control of us,** and it dictated most our thoughts.

Third, when in survival mode, **the priority is always urgency.** Everything is reactive actions.

Fourth, when in survival mode, and married, **for better or worse is just a nightmare with unicorns as the monsters.** It seems pretty in appearance and a beast when you finally walk in the woods.

Fifth, when in survival mode, **your level of ignorance will determine your place in society.** We were a working poor, middle-class family, trying to make ends meet because of our ignorance. We embraced lessons learned and not learned from our upbringings. We had a survivor's mindset. We were living in survivor's mode.

Several years later there was a shift to living in abundance...

Being a holistic life and business coach, I target finances as my starting point with clients to provide them the tools and techniques to effectively elevate their minds, leverage their finances, be their own boss so that they can leave a legacy behind and not a liability. This is my company's slogan and my personal mantra. **Legacy** is a holistic word and requires holistic thinking and actions.

Presently, you can find me speaking at community events on spiritual warfare, finances and mental health awareness. Surprisingly, each has many parallels.

In the beginning of my breakthrough, I felt like Moses. Why would anyone listen to me? I had the worst financial history. God's reply was, "That is exactly why I am using you!"

Though I've encountered, equipped and empowered many people to do better with their finances by changing their mindset to an abundant one, I still am amazed at the many things I learn about people and their relationship with money. The most common two things I've learned is that most of my clients:

1. Want to do better and just don't know where to start or how to start to get on that road of financial freedom.
2. Don't have the foundation to build off when it comes to an abundant mindset.

What does your legacy look like? If you were to die today, would you leave behind a liability? Or a legacy that someone, specifically a family member, friend, or someone in your community can pick up the torch and carry on what you've started?

I have many favorite scriptures in the Bible, but two that I often speak of regarding finances is John 10:10 and Deuteronomy 8:18.

John 10:10, "The thief comes to steal and kill and destroy; I came that YOU may have life, and have it abundantly".
More often than not, as experienced and witnessed, people are the robbers of their own wealth, progress, and purpose. God has called us to live abundant lives, and that abundance includes wealth. Keep in mind that wealth is not totally a dollar sign. Wealth is applied knowledge that turns into wisdom, and is lived out in a prosperous life through obedience and discipline.

Deuteronomy 8:18, "But remember the LORD your God, for it is he who gives YOU the ABILITY to produce wealth, and so confirms his covenant, which he swore to your ancestors, as it is today".

The ability to produce wealth comes from knowledge of knowing how to obtain, sustain and reproduce wealth, not just for yourself, but for others. It costs to feed the poor, so if you ARE poor, you are costly and costing others. You can't be poor and be operating in your purpose because poor is holistic.

So, how does one avoid or get out of a survivor's mindset and living in a survivor's mode when it comes to finances?

Great question!

First, understand and comprehend the definition of a **survivor's mindset**. You will not find this definition in a dictionary. The meaning of this phrase has been developed from personal experience and having my client's experience the same lifestyle and mindset.

Survivors Mindset is being in a place where you are the thief to your own progress and process. It is a state of thinking and acting in terms of the RIGHT NOW.

Think about the behaviors of a common petty thief or someone who lives paycheck-to-paycheck. The situation that got them in their current predicament is irrelevant. However, while the thief is robbing others, the person living paycheck-to-paycheck is robbing themselves and/or their family. They are thieves of their own progress and process. When you equate this to finances, it is easy to see how many people are in the category of poor or working poor.

According to the U.S. Bureau of Labor Statistics, about 9.5 million people who spent at least 27 weeks in the labor force were poor. The Center for Poverty Research, University of California, Davis cited that in 2014, the working poor were:

- 11.7% Black, 11.7% Hispanic/Latino, 5.5% White, 4.3% Asian
  - 7.2% women, 5.5% men
  - 18.3% with less than a high school diploma
  - 8.3% high school graduates with no college education
  - 2% with a bachelor's degree or higher

It doesn't matter how you slice the statistics, the fact of the matter is that the survivor's mindset is an equal opportunity beast, and many are its prey!

Use these wisdom tidbits to get out of the claws of the survivor's mindset.

Breaking the cycle of a survivor's mindset...and on to abundance

1.   **Be aware of poor financial behaviors**, such as spending too much eating out, buying unnecessary items before paying your bills, not knowing where your money is going to, or emotional spending. Extreme behaviors include, but are not limited to: gambling, spending more than $100 dollars on online or video games, spending money on pornography. (Be real and honest about your spending). **Once you identify your poor financial hiccups, make every attempt to eliminate them**! Most professionals and authors note that it takes 30 days to break a habit. So start today!

What are your poor financial behaviors? Write them down...now to get a clear picture of what it is costing you!

Describe your upbringing when it comes to finances. Did your parents teach you the principles of savings and obtaining wealth? Was it even a conversation?

2.   **Create a budget. Update your budget. Stick to your budget as much as possible**. Warren Buffet, Oprah Winfrey, and 50 Cent did not become wealthy because they didn't know where their money was going. Trust and believe, they know where 95% if not, 100% of their money is going. *An effective budget will tell you where your money is going one to six months out or more, depending on how far in advance you plan.* It can also provide you a simple picture of your **debt-to-income-ratio (or DIT)**. A DIT ratio is how much money you have versus how much in expenses you have. If you have more expenses than income, your DIT is high or in the red. If you have more money than expenses, your DIT is probably in the green. However, if you are not managing your finances correctly, regardless of how much money you have you can still experience a survivor's mindset and be broke. There are many billionaires and millionaires that are broke.

60

a.   Your budget will need to include all your incomes. Anything you are using to pay your expenses per month. This includes regular payroll, disability, child support, etc.

b.   Your expenses include all the necessary items required to maintain your household. Understand that Netflix is not required to maintain your household. That is a luxury item. If you can't afford it, get rid of it.

Do you have a budget? Is it active? What is your total income for the month? What are your total expenses, excluding items on your credit report? If it's on your credit report, it is not an expense, it is a debt.

If you need a starter budget to get the ball rolling, continue reading to the end. I got you covered!

ALERT! If you are a business owner, most small businesses fail in less than two years due to inadequate cash reserves. If you have poor financial habits, more times than not, those same financial behaviors you have in your personal life, crossover into your business finances.

3.   **Establish an emergency budget!** Popular authors and financial gurus like Dave Ramsey recommend that you start your emergency savings with at least $1000. I agree. However, I understand that everyone is not equipped or able. Start with what you can, even if it's $25 dollars. Something is better than nothing. Better to build with concentrate on a sunny day, than to stand in mud while it rains.

4.   **Create short and long-term financial goals.**
Do you desire to purchase a home in the future? What about a car?

Do you want to retire early, instead of waiting until society's standard retirement age?

Would you like to have college funds saved for your children or grandchildren?

Would you like to have great credit for maximized purchasing power?

Would you like to give monies to charities and churches stress-free?

Would you like to start your own business?

Would you like to teach your children or grandchildren how to manage money?

Would you like to help your parents out financially?

Would you like to go on a vacation hassle-free?

Would you like to pay for unexpected emergencies like your car breaking down, or a medical bill without having to tap into your regular income?

Would you like to learn how to invest money effectively?

Would you like to live each day forgetting like it's a payday because your finances are in order?

Write your financial goals down! Make it plain. Read them every day or once a week. Put them into action!

5.   **Educate yourself about financial growth and wealth**. My people perish because of lack of knowledge is a powerful scripture in the Bible and can reference everything in life, especially money. Financial education is an absolute must and there are numerous websites that offer FREE information. **Mine is one of them, keep reading**. Some of most wealthy people live simple lives! Look at Mark Zuckerberg or Keanu Reeves. They don't dress all flashy or buy unnecessary expensive items. I have personally witnessed many people, including clients that have worn more money on them in name brand labels as compared to what is in their bank account.

Things that make you go hmmmmm…..

6.   **Whether you are single, in a relationship, or married, everyone must be on the same sheet of music when it comes to**

finances if living under the same roof. I've witnessed many couples with different philosophies about finances, as well as different behaviors. When two people from two different backgrounds and upbringings come together to co-exist in the same space, money is generally a fighting factor, right under miscommunication. Like everything in a relationship, finances need to be discussed and planned together.

**Abundance Mindset** means being spiritually, mentally, and physically equipped for famine circumstances when they arrive (having cash reserves and being consciously aware of your financial status); able to effectively maintain your household and being able to assist in the community that you live in, to the point that your assistance does not inadequately take food off your table. Having the wisdom to leave a legacy behind, and not a liability, for your children's children.

**Are you ready to embrace the abundant life that God speaks of?**

**Are you ready to have an Abundance Mindset?**

Today is the day you say enough is enough with the survivor's mindset and behaviors! Grab ahold of the abundance that is waiting for you NOW! Download the FREE Budgeting and Blessings Workbook, which includes a starter budget at https://www.subscribepage.com/CoachRedMoneyCodeBook

Nicole "Coach Red" Redmond is the Owner and CEO of Redmond Legacy Coaching, LLC. She is a Holistic Life and Business Coach, visionary, and financial strategist. She does not claim to be a financial guru. Just someone who has endured many trials and triumphs when it comes to mindsight, money and life, in general. Redmond Legacy Coaching, LLC is geared to position people not conform to the commonalities of unfavorable economic circumstances, such as living paycheck-to-paycheck, poor credit worthiness, unhealthy financial and life habits, inadequate savings, and ineffective business operations which impacts households and business ownership. Instead to transform, elevate, and equip people with effective strategies that will enable them to leave a legacy behind a not a liability.

She loves reading books, writing poetry, and spoken word. Traveling internationally with her husband or her sister social circle and experiencing different cultures is a passion. She is fascinated with the psychology of people's behaviors. She also loves traveling with her teenage daughter and trying our different restaurants. They are genuine foodies. She has a Master's of Science in Psychology, and a Bachelor's of Science in Management Information Systems.

You can contact her today:
Facebook:https://www.facebook.com/RedmondLegacyCoaching/
IG: https://www.instagram.com/coachredrlc/
Website: www.redmondlegacycoaching.com
Email: CoachRed@redmondlegacycoaching.com

Chapter Six
Healing to Get Results
~Jennifer Stephanie Alvarez~

There was a time when I was using the power of my subconscious mind to create everything I didn't want.

I was in a verbally abusive relationship with an alcoholic.

I lost my house - A house that I visited monthly as it was being built so that I could envision all of the wonderful memories I was going to create in there.

My credit score was horrible.

I had no savings to speak of, I was in debt, and on top of all of that, my account was overdrawn.

My mortgage business was failing due to changes in the market.

I was unhealthy and overweight.

And then I found out I was pregnant.

To sum it all up, I was depressed.

This was a new state of being for me because I'd been a fairly positive person. But with everything going on, I really thought that I had hit rock bottom. Especially as the conditions of my abusive relationship got worse as he was drinking more.

As I got further into my pregnancy, I was diagnosed with gestational diabetes and needed insulin shots. But as the breadwinner, I was still working to close deals in my business, and I had even been working in the hospital right up until the moment that I suffered from preeclampsia and had an emergency C-section after being in labor for 2 days. And even after my daughter was born I found myself having anxiety attacks that were so bad, with each one I thought that I was going to die.

One day, her dad was preoccupied with 2 tall cans of Budweiser and I remember he was really upset about a package of pictures I bought. He berated me relentlessly about spending money and nothing I said or did seemed to stop him. It was a rough time, facing a financial stressor from buying something as simple as a pack of pictures.

I went on doing everything I could to sustain financially for a couple more years, until there came a time when I couldn't do it any longer.

A friend told me a major bank was hiring and I told my daughter's father that he should apply. But we actually both ended up applying because I found out that I could work and still do loans on the side with no issues.

Just when it looked like our financial strain would be relieved and maybe even our relationship, another bombshell hit.

I found out that while I was doing everything I could to support our family; he was spending his time cheating with not one, but two women.

Needless to say, I was distraught.

Especially to find that one of the women worked in the bank with us, and I was in a leadership role over her.

While I thought I was depressed before, these were truly some dark times for me financially AND emotionally.

I remember times when I would go into the bathroom and cry during work. It took everything in me to put on a "happy" face because it felt like I was dying on the inside. It was clear that my 12 year relationship with someone who was once my best friend had failed.

I was mourning the loss of the dream I had growing up, being happily married and raising my child in a two parent household. And after the relationship was over, I went through an even deeper level of depression and it took everything in me to get out of bed every day and raise our daughter.

I remembered when I started working at that job I had a vision of climbing the corporate ladder quickly and helping other women do the same thing. The vision grew and expanded while my life was falling apart and it was that vision that helped me get through it.

I wanted a better life for my daughter and I was determined to succeed.

I knew deep down this was all happening for a reason and no matter what, I was going to get through it because on the other end was access to all of my dreams.

I allowed myself to mourn and grieve the relationship. I worked on forgiving him and myself because I felt like I betrayed myself after seeing so many red flags. I began to focus on everything I could control. I have been on a journey my whole life to find the deeper meaning of life and become the best possible version of myself.

So I began to immerse myself in the journey.

I started to take care of myself by working out and eating healthy. I started a meditation practice. I went to many different healers and began practicing the healing modality I was trained in years earlier. I repaired my credit. I started to save for retirement. I started to pay off my debts. I started to use the energy we all have available and I became very purposeful with how I used it. I mastered my mind and the money, the lifestyle, the dream became a reality. I am now an internationally best selling author, speaker, consultant, producer and co-host of a nationally syndicated show, and travel journalist who gets paid to play. I also work with other people and help them make their dream life a reality.

During that time I learned many things.

I learned to always listen to my intuition. It had warned me many times about that relationship and what was going on. I realized everybody has the power within them to change their lives. As humans we create things twice, once in our mind, and again in reality. We can use the Universal energy from the formless realm and bring it into our material world. This energy is limitless. We can use it to create more money in our lives and a lifestyle filled with health, happiness, peace, amazing memories, laughter, love, more time with our family, successful careers and businesses. The possibilities are limitless.

I want to share with you how I used the power within me to bring my thoughts into form.

Focus on what YOU want.

I often ask people what they want and they tell me everything they don't want. They say things like "I don't want to live paycheck to paycheck". The key is to focus on what you want. Use the power of your subconscious which is 30,000 times more powerful than our conscious.

Ask yourself questions like, "How can I afford that? How can I help more people and earn more money in my business? How can I get paid to travel the world?"

This is important because our reality is determined by the questions we ask ourselves.

Ask powerful questions and let your subconscious go to work on the answers. I journal affirmations about how I want my life to be. I use the power of my imagination by meditating about my dream life and how I want to feel for at least 5 minutes a day. Our subconscious can't tell the difference between what we are imagining and what is real.

I practice forgiving others and myself. There was a time I hated my ex until I realized he's doing the best he can with the tools he has.

And guess what, we all are.

I realized the hardest person to forgive was myself. I had to release the shame I felt about my story and everything I let happen. But, I never gave up.

Through my journey, I learned to use the lessons I learned to create the life I wanted. And with these same tools, you too can attract more money in your life, have more freedom and let your spirit soar.

To take things to the next level, download a free Money Meditation at www.themoneyhealer.com

And to stay connected, visit me on FaceBook Instagram and LinkedIN at The Money Healer.

Stephanie J. Alvarez also known as The Money Healer , serves and supports holistic business owners, conscious entrepreneurs, healers, coaches, and corporate employees to achieve the freedom they desire and deserve. With over twelve years as a financial industry veteran, Native Medicine Carrier, and Wisdom Carrier, Stephanie brings a unique balance of practical and spiritual experience to provide her clients with a holistic approach to living a life of freedom. Stephanie is a current member of the Personal Finance Speakers Association and recently spoke at the Microsoft LinkedIn event to help business owners achieve financial freedom.

She is currently the President for the Holistic Chamber of Commerce in Brentwood CA, a Certified Financial Education Instructor, Certified Identity Theft Risk Management Specialist, Licensed Real Estate Salesperson, and Licensed Life & Health Insurance agent, co-author of the international best seller, "The Missing Piece in Gratitude and Abundance".

Chapter Seven
Make, Maintain & Multiply Your Money with Powerful Language
~Gemma James~

It sounds like a totally cheesy way to start my section of this book but...... I remember the day as if it were yesterday.

It was a cold, wet Friday. I had loaded up my basket with groceries and I was at the self-checkout. Basket, baby, bags and in a rush. I'd already tried my PIN Number twice but, sweating and feeling myself getting redder and redder I tried it again....the same response came up.

'Payment Not Accepted'.

'Must be a fault with my card' I could hear myself saying out loud as it felt like every pair of eyes in the store was on me. But I knew EXACTLY what the problem was.

I didn't have enough money in my account.

I'd been struggling with money for a LONG time. I always had to plan, move money around, say no to treats, stress about where money was going to come from and don't even get me started on Christmas! I felt like I'd been drowning in debt forever.

But it had never been this bad. I'd never been unable to buy my family food before....

It was totally embarrassing, deflating and very upsetting.

I was sweating and almost in tears as I was forced to leave the bags at the checkout and leave the store.

That day was pretty much rock bottom for me. As I walked home with my baby under my arm and my food still at the store, I thought about my life until that point. About the decisions I had made regarding money, the times I had spent when I should have saved, the times when I'd maxed out my credit cards on things I probably didn't really NEED but justified buying anyway and I thought about my ability to make money and my deservingness of it.

My discovery?

I'd been pretty shitty to myself, I'd been pretty shitty to money and as a result, money had been pretty shitty to me.

I made the decision to change on that walk home.

I had friends who had saved for holidays and deposits for homes while I had just gone deeper and deeper into debt. I knew there were so many people in the world who had a fantastic relationship with money so I knew it was possible....and I decided there and then that it was possible for me too!

And do you know what? It's totally possible for you too....

Let's cut to today and I'm now writing this from my office in the beautiful new home I recently manifested (and put down a year's rent up front in cash!). I run my own business from home around my beautiful family, I've cleared off half of the 20k of credit card debt and I'm living a life that FEELS so much more abundant every single day.

Do you want to know how I turned it around?

I learned about the power of our mindset.

<u>Sounds a bit 'Rainbows and Unicorns' right?</u>

I know, but trust me, your language and the way you speak to yourself and others can have a HUGE effect on your ability to actually make, maintain and multiply your money.

You may have heard before the phrase *'what you focus on you attract'* and there is actually a reason behind it. There's a part of your brain that filters in the information that we feed it. We are inundated with so much information every minute of the day that we would probably all go insane if we didn't have this filtering process in place. So the way the brain knows what to filter, is by the things we are focusing on – all the stuff we are thinking about, talking about and acting on. It's then going to do everything in its power to bring those things into your reality. (That's where the word 'Manifest' comes from – it simply means to 'make real'). You're bringing into your reality all those things that you're focusing on. Your brain doesn't understand the difference between what is actually 'good' or 'bad' or what is right for you or wrong for you, it literally acts on what you tell it.

This is why your language can have such a powerful effect on your success with money. When you can use your language in such a way that your brain picks up on it, focuses on it, filters it and works its ass off to bring those things into your reality, it can bring you more of those things that make you feel good, give you more confidence and your success with money is going to soar!

Mind Your Language!

So a great way to start changing the way you think and talk is to be really mindful of your language. I'm not talking about trying not to swear, this isn't about that. I'm talking about really being mindful of the words and phrases that you use. Because there are certain words that can actually limit your chances of success and your potential. This is how your brain is going to build certain beliefs and limitations within you.

So, if for example, you find yourself frequently saying things like:

"I can't…"
"I won't…"

"I shouldn't…"
"I'll never be able to…"

…these are really limiting phrases. Your brain is going to pick up on that and your limitations will be set. You've told yourself time and time again that you can't do something for example, so your brain won't actually ALLOW you to do it. That pesky comfort zone is going to kick in (eye roll) and you might find that you always seem to reach a certain point and then never get any further. Or maybe your money seems to leave you as quick as it arrives. And like I said earlier, the more you focus on something (*"I hate being in so much debt"*) the more your brain is going to respond to that and bring you more of those things (more debt – eye roll again).

Other words and phrases that can be detrimental to your success with money are tricky little sneaky ones. On the surface they appear positive, because you're talking about things you want to achieve, and so you would think that they would be great to use right?
Actually, no….

I'm talking about *"hopefully"*, *"someday"*, *"one day"* and *"I'll try"*. Although these all seem lovely and fluffy on the outside, they still suggest some doubt to your subconscious that you can ACTUALLY achieve what it is you're talking about.

For Example:

"Hopefully" translates to, *"I'm not sure if I can but it would be quite nice if I could, but I probably can't, but I don't want to appear negative so I'll come up with a nicer word instead..."*

"One day" becomes, *"I'm not sure if I can so I'll just keep putting it off until I'm absolutely certain and I've perfected everything and I'm absolutely really REALLY clear and sure that I can and then I will, but until then I'll just keep talking about it..."*
"Someday" is more along the lines of *"[being the same as 'One Day' but add even longer to keep talking about it]"*

"I'll try" is just plain, *"I'm not sure if I can and I probably can't but I don't want to appear negative and just give up right away so if I look like I'm giving it a go then I can give up in a little bit and not feel bad because I gave it a go..."*

I'm going to let you in on a secret ok?

Ready?

Ok here goes...

'ONE DAY' AND 'SOMEDAY' ARE NEVER GOING TO HAPPEN!

Your brain loves specificity! 'One day' and 'someday' is too vague.

Instead, when talking about your goals, things you want to achieve, your feelings about money etc, aim to use sentences that begin:

"I am"
"I will"
"I can"

This will tell your brain that there is no doubt in your mind that you <u>can</u> and <u>will</u> achieve your goals (increase your income, save better etc.) – even if you don't necessarily believe it to begin with!

It's only human to want to say 'hopefully' as we don't want to come across as cocky or sure of ourselves and so we say hopefully. But be mindful of it and change your language when you pick up on it.

Just so we're clear, I'm not saying that as soon as you say *"I will make 1k this month"* the sky will open up and crisp fresh notes will come floating down into your lap!

But it's about having unwavering faith that everything is going to work out for you, understanding that there are no limitations upon

75

you other than the ones you set upon yourself. So when you break down those barriers and change those *"I can'ts" "I won'ts"* and **"I'll never be able to's"** to **"I am"**, **"I can"** and **"I will"** and you lose the *"hopefully's"*, you'll find yourself in a more positive state of mind, you'll feel more confident and your bank balance will get a boost - because your brain will pick up on those things you're talking about, and the more specific you can be, the more likely it is that your brain will bring them into your reality.

Once More With Feeling!!!

There is a way that you can really start to break down those limitations and barriers, create more positive language and as a result bring more positive things into your life and that is with the use of affirmations.

Affirmations have been absolutely HUGE for me and have been so beneficial to my success with and attitude towards money.
I love them because they are so simple to use but when used correctly can supercharge your success!

Very simply, Affirmations are positive statements that you tell yourself that really reaffirms your confidence and belief in what is available and attainable to you. You can speak them out loud, put them on the wall, think about them or write them in a journal, whatever works for you. But there are **two main points** to remember to achieve the most success with using them.

1. **Repetition and habit is key.**
   For Affirmations to have any sort of effect you need to be repeating them over and over again. I don't mean sitting in a Yoga position chanting them for hours on end but they will absolutely not work if you don't build up the habit. This isn't a 'magic spell' where you say it once and you're magically transformed. For habits to form it can take 28 days of consistent action and so at the minimum you should be repeating your affirmations once a day, especially to begin with when installing these new habits into your daily life. After a while you'll realize that you either don't feel you need

them (because you've achieved what you wanted and so you'll move on to the next one) or that they just become so habitual that they're as natural to you as brushing your teeth.

2. **<u>Get into the feelz</u>** (yeah I totally went there...)
   You may have heard about standing in front of the mirror in a Superhero pose or maybe can recall the Friends Episode (Season 6 Episode 22 in case you want to check it out) where Bruce Willis is the 'Love Machine' in 'The One Where Paul's The Man' (essentially this was him using Affirmations!) and you can absolutely do this if you wish.

   HOWEVER I assure you that if the thought of talking to yourself in the mirror (or Bruce's Love Machine dance...) makes you cringe then this is NOT a requirement for successful Affirmations. The MOST IMPORTANT THING is the feeling. Your brain responds to your emotions over everything else and so more important than what you say and where you say it, is the feeling you give to it while doing it.

   This may be difficult to start with if you're new to this, if you're used to using fairly limiting language and if it still feels weird to be telling yourself how awesome you are (you are by the way!) then 'fake it' until you get it. As soon as you start saying them regularly, your brain will pick up on it and it will feel so much easier and more natural and will soon become a part of your daily life.

So as I stated above, you absolutely do not need to be standing in a superhero pose in front of the mirror for these to work – though you absolutely can. This is about finding what works for you. These will be a personal thing to you and what works for you may not work for me and vice versa. The best way I can advise to start adding Affirmations into your life so they become part of your daily routine and you find your own 'flow' with them is to use Triggers. These will be little things you do going about your day that will remind you to say them. Or remind you of the feeling they give you to take you back to that feeling, even for just a second.

It might be, for example, that you repeat your affirmations to yourself every time you jump in the shower or think about them every time you brush your teeth. It might be every time you're brushing your hair or putting your make up on that you finish with a badass Wonder Woman pose and spend 30 seconds saying them.

One way that worked really well for me was to set an alarm on your phone to go off every few hours with either the whole Affirmation (depending on how long it is) or one or two key words in there. This will remind you to say them, think about them, or focus on the feeling they give you.

You could also set your own Triggers of every time you see a purple flower or a white butterfly or walk across a drain cover – whatever it is, you get the idea. Find what works for YOU.

Whatever you set as your Triggers, these will make your brain kick into gear again. If you can be thinking about it and talking about it as much as possible it will jumpstart that filtering process and you'll be on the lookout (without you knowing it) for more of those things to come into your life.

And like I said before, the most important thing is you add in that emotion.

How does it feel when you say it, when it gives you that level of success or the income that you want? Think about the money coming into your bank account, that figure growing, the treats and not having to worry about the bills. The feelings are about more than just the word.

Action Step
Start to think about how you can get some Affirmations into your life with the use of Triggers. Note down some times when you could spend even just 30 seconds doing them. Set up some alarms in your phone if that's what you want to do. You'll soon see how you can easily add Affirmations into your life AT LEAST once a day.

I know this may seem like a complete waste of time but this is absolutely where your journey to success with money will begin. It's getting you that confidence and self-belief, productivity and positivity and they have helped me to increase my income, save better, invest wisely, manifest free lunches and awesome relationships and very recently my dream house AND the furniture to go in it! So give it a go, what have you got to lose right?

So I know by now you may be thinking 'well this is all great, but what do I actually say?!' This is really down to you and the goals you want to achieve. There is no 'one size fits all' rule when it comes to Affirmations and like I said before, it's more important the feeling you get when you say it than the words you actually use. However, the most effective positive language will be phrases and sentences that start with 'I am,' 'I will' and 'I can' right? So certainly these are a good place to start. Your Affirmations can be short snappy sentences such as:

'I am confident'
'I am fabulous with money'
'I am a money magnet'
'I can easily multiply my money'

Or they can be longer sentences and phrases. One that I used over and over again when I was getting started (and still use to this day when I need to) is:

'I give amazing value and I get amazing value back in return. I am so blessed and grateful that I have this amazing gift that allows me to make massive amounts of income for me and my family and massive amounts of impact on people all over the world so that they can do the same, so that we all are living our dream lifestyles. Thank you Universe for the abundance that flows into my life every single day filling my heart and my bank account with absolute joy'.

Yours does not need to be that long. Do what feels right to you. Put them into your own language and words so they feel natural to you and remember, add in the FEELING!

Action Step
If you're struggling to come up with some Affirmations then a great way to start is to turn around the words, thoughts and opinions

you already have so they serve you better. The point of Affirmations and powerful language is to retrain your brain so that you focus on the awesome stuff and repel the bad, not the other way round.

Take at least 15 minutes to complete the following exercise. Somewhere you can concentrate distraction free. The best way I find to do this exercise is with good old paper and pen and not on the computer or your phone so make sure you have that ready before you begin.

Step 1: Think about a goal you want to achieve. Something you would absolutely love to come true (hint: not just one that you think is possible). This doesn't have to be a big scary goal like become a millionaire by the time you're 50 or anything like that (and in fact it is better if it's not to begin with) but might be 'I want to make an extra 1k a month'. Or 'I want to save 5k next year' or 'I want to take my family to Disney Land'. Be as specific with it as possible (it is not enough to just want to be 'richer' or 'happier'). Choose a specific goal and then note it down.

Step 2: Immediately as soon as you have thought of it and written it down, then underneath write down EVERYTHING that comes to mind. An absolute brain dump kind of thing. Don't analyze, don't judge, don't question if you're doing it right, don't leave anything off because you think it's not important, literally EVERYTHING that comes to mind when you think of that goal. Spend at least 2 minutes on this or until you have nothing left.

This may go something like this:

Goal:

I want to make 3k next month

Thoughts:

But who am I even kidding

Maybe I should have written 2k

80

I've never even reached 2k before so why would I get to 3?

How would I even do that?

Could I sell some stuff?

That would be amazing if I hit 3k!

I'd totally go shopping!

Ooh I could get that new top in that ridiculously expensive store

I don't know why I'm thinking about what I'd buy when I haven't even got it yet

What's the point of this again?

I don't think I'm doing this right

This probably isn't for me

I'm just not one of the lucky ones

I guess my job isn't that bad

Noodles every day for dinner is better than nothing

This is not going to be possible for me

You get the idea right?!
Now it's your turn

<u>Step 3:</u>

Go through your 'brain dump' from Step 2 and pick out all of the negative ones. All the ones where you've questioned whether it's possible or told yourself it won't work or wondered how etc. Then once you have those, choose just 3. Whichever 3 stand out to you the most. Don't spend too long thinking about it; just go with your instincts.

Step 4:

Turn those 3 negative statements into a positive. Again put them into your own words and language so they feel natural to you but as an example:

Negative statement from Brain Dump – 'That's not even possible'

New Positive Statement – 'It is more than possible for me to bring in the income I desire'

Negative statement from Brain Dump – 'But I'm so rubbish with money'

New Positive Statement – 'I love money and money loves me! I easily and effortlessly save money every month'

Do this with all 3 of your negative statements and congrats! You now have your new positive Affirmations.

Say them daily, believe them when you say it and tune into the FEELING!

To Your Success!!

For even more tips on how to add powerful (and successful) Affirmations into your daily life, head to http://bit.ly/MoneyBookAffirmations for FREE access to my Powerful Affirmations Implementation Toolkit or to get in touch (I'd love for you to share your new powerful affirmations!) email me at gemmajameshc@gmail.com

Gemma is an Advanced Law of Attraction Practitioner, Wealth Practitioner, Happiness Coach, Course Creator, Author, Mum, wife and chocolate lover....phew!

Long story short, she used to live in a place of scarcity and lack. Then she learnt some awesome things about the power of our brains, our language and our mindset and it is now her passion to help others create their dream life and live out the best version of themselves, by breaking through their barriers and limitations, to change what is possible with powerful language (that's kind of her super power...) and to live happier, wealthier and more abundantly in all aspects.

She dreamed of being an author since she was old enough to hold a pen and she's grateful that not only has one of her own dreams now been fulfilled, but she also gets to impact the world with her books so that others can create their dreams too

.

Chapter Eight
You Were Put On This Earth to Thrive Not Simply Survive
~Dominique Mullally~

For most of us, especially women, money is a hot topic. It's a topic wrapped up in shame, guilt, anger, frustration and anxiety.

Sound familiar?

So why is it that we are far more comfortable talking with our girlfriends about how much sex we're getting than we are talking about how much money we're receiving? I know you know what I'm talking about!

At the end of the day, money is a tool....something we simply use in exchange for something we want, for something we value yet the sheer mention of the word money is enough for some of us to turn our stomach or have crippling pangs of anxiety.

Trust me though; it doesn't have to be this way.

I want to tell you my story first so you can understand why it is that I can sit here and 'tell' you about money. Firstly I want you to know, my aim is not to just 'tell' you... my aim is to educate and empower you. To give you the courage to take back control of your money and take out the emotional charge you may currently be feeling and have the confidence to know that the power to change your current financial situation lies within you!!

I may be empowered now with regard to my money but it wasn't always that way! I personally under-earned for many years......all because someone very close to me had told me that a man would not want to be with a woman who was more financially successful than them. That it would emasculate them and they would eventually leave.

Unconsciously I truly believed this! I mean why wouldn't I, that was the only thing I had continuously heard and I didn't have anything or anyone to challenge that belief so I lived it as if it was real.

I was in a role with an uncapped bonus and yet every month without fail, I'd hit that glass ceiling. It was almost like an invisible barrier month after month that stopped me from breaking into that next level of income. I'd resist it…I would literally resist earning more money. I didn't know it at the time but that belief had set a predetermined amount that I was 'comfortable' with. An amount of money

I knew I'd stay safe at, and my partner would be comfortable with and because these beliefs were 'real' to me, that meant I'd not become more financially successful than him and have him leave me.

It was a continuous pattern of self-sabotage.

As crazy as this sounds this is how our subconscious mind…where these beliefs live….works! Its only job is to keep us safe and alive. We've evolved so much emotionally as humans but our subconscious minds are still very primitive.

When I became a Financial Adviser, I began to see a real difference in the way men and women handle their money affairs. Men were very matter of fact, unapologetic about their desire to create more wealth. Most women, the complete opposite, emotional about their money and apologetic about the very same thing that men made no apologies for…but why?

We have somehow allowed the income we earn or the money we do or don't have, to somehow define us and who we really are. Since when did we allow a measure of our self-worth to be stacked up in numbers? And why are we resisting gaining more control and receiving more money into our lives?

Now I know even as you're reading this book, some of you are going to feel resistance at some points throughout the different chapters.

That's good!

It confirms you have some fears around money.

I repeat, this is good - because the first step to change is acknowledgement. We want your fear to come to the surface so you can recognize it, acknowledge it, and push through anyway. So remember the words of Susan Jefferson as you read through these chapters 'Feel the fear and do it anyway'.

Working on mastering the emotional side of money can feel like hard work, like there's a resistance to getting that clarity and pushing forward to take back that control. That's because we crave what's familiar and comfortable.........but we know what's familiar and comfortable doesn't serve you nor pay your bills.... I mean it might....but sometimes just barely.

Resistance comes in different forms like:
- You lose interest
- You get distracted
- You can't be bothered
- You don't have time
- You are paralyzed
- You feel overwhelmed

Some of these signs might be coming up for you even as you read this book. But here's what I know. Resistance really masks fear. It may be fear of the unknown, fear of letting go, fear of stepping into your greatness. Who knows, since fear is different and very real for each one of us.

There is a lot of fear around money, most times the fear is that there simply is not enough money, but for women it shifts into, 'I'm not enough'. Usually as women at the core of our beliefs is this notion that we are somehow not deserving of more. Be it more money, more love, just more abundance.

I know it can feel scary, and overwhelming and like hard work, facing up to some of this stuff but I can PROMISE YOU, you'll feel so much better once you push through that resistance and onto the other side.

At the end of the day, to get different results you have to do things differently and that can feel uncomfortable. Really uncomfortable, but what's more uncomfortable facing up to how you really feel about where you currently are and working on changing that or continuing this financial path and ending up even more stuck financially than you might already be? It's all about taking back control and making a different choice.

I want you to know that it's ok to give yourself the permission of choice and to change things. Yes I say permission because as women we're the caretakers and we take care of everyone else spiritually, emotionally, financially before we take care of ourselves. We will run on empty just to ensure no one else goes hungry, literally and figuratively speaking but at the end of the day you can't give from an empty cup and it isn't noble to remain broke or struggling to just get by. It doesn't mean you're a better person because you sacrifice. It just means your focus becomes surviving instead of thriving.

Facing up to the facts of where you are financially right now might feel uncomfortable but it's necessary to take off the money blinders and clearly see where you need to go and what steps you need to take to get you there.

Remember mastering your money emotions and identifying the beliefs that drive them is key to your financial and spiritual growth.

In every situation, even the unhelpful, unhealthy ones, as crazy as it sounds, there is a payoff.

I know you're probably thinking, wait what?! Like is this girl crazy??!! Yes…maybe…occasionally but when it comes to the talk of money…never! There is a reason why you are not progressing financially and seem to be stuck in the same pattern of behaviors and habits.

For me it was because potentially by upgrading my income, I would lose my partner at the time. To say it out loud it's like, girl please but in my unconscious head, it was a big fat reality!

Exercise 1 – By being in your current financial situation, what is the pay off? What is there to gain by your current financial situation? What is there to lose by changing it?

Close your eyes, ask yourself this question and pay attention to what comes up.

Notice what comes up. This is the one thing we must work on to break the habit to give yourself the permission to change things.

Now I don't want you to be so hard on yourself, your financial situation is not your fault. I repeat it's not your fault. Your money mindset (which I'll explain in a minute) is just stuck on a non-supportive setting… but just as easily as you learned those unhelpful beliefs and habits you can so easily unlearn them…trust me!

So let's talk about money.

See here's the thing, money is an energy.

We are simply a conduit, a vessel for that energy. So depending on the emotional energy you put into money, it determines what you get back. It's a cycle of loop the loop!

We become so emotionally attached to our money we allow it to become an extension of who we are. It affects how we show up and what we do in the world.

So let's begin to take the sting out of it.

How would it feel if for the next 24hrs, you replaced the word money, for the word energy? Instead of saying I have no money say, I have no energy.

What do you notice when you replace the word money with another word? How does it feel? I'm guessing it felt a lot less intense....like there was no or very little emotional charge behind that word that you used to replace it with.

Remember, YOU are in control....at all times. It may seem from time to time that you find yourself in a tail spin and you wake up in cold sweats or dread opening your bills but that's because you feel you have no power and power, comes from clarity.

Your money mindset is the key to your overall financial situation. Your money mindset is a formation of your deepest beliefs about money and this affects how we feel, how we act and what we do with money. Beliefs are formed in our early years by experiences.......things we heard, saw or felt about money indirectly or directly. Once formed we live these beliefs as though they are real...and for most of us they are!

So let's find out...... what some of your beliefs are!

Exercise 1 – What did your parents/grandparents say about money, how did they feel about people with money?

On a scale of 1-10 (with 10 being off the scale) how real do these beliefs feel for you?

Once you've identified your beliefs I want you to pretend you're a lawyer arguing the case for the other side, the side which dispels these beliefs. What evidence can you find all around you to prove these beliefs could be wrong?

90

See, your financial situation today is merely an outcome of these unseen beliefs which are wrapped up in many different symptoms. These beliefs drive how we feel about money, that's why it's so emotional for us.

They manifest themselves in different ways but this is what they may look like:
- Under-earning
- Undercharging
- Overspending
- Living in a continuous state of feast or feminine
- Having little or no savings
- Being unable to break the cycle of debt

Because we experience the world with senses (well for those of us that are fortunate) we hear money language every day. You can usually tell someone's money mindset by how they speak.

It may sound like:
- I can't afford that
- That's too expensive
- Money don't grow on trees
- You can be rich or you can be spiritual but you can't be both
- It is better to give than it is to receive

And lastly, because most of us are emotional about money and we respond according to our feelings. This is how it may feel for us:
- Anxious
- Worried
- Embarrassed
- Shameful
- Guilty
- Resentful
- Desperate

As crazy as this sounds, these are our comfort zones with money, they are habitual behaviors that we repeat over and over again. Like a hamster on that wheel, we will continue to run in circles until we make a conscious decision to get off!

Getting clarity is the first step.

So let's determine our emotional drives first:
1. What words in your own language represent how you feel about money, or those with money?
2. What are your go to phrases around money, things you find yourself saying a lot?
3. How are these words and phrases manifesting in your current financial situation?

Now that you have identified your current emotional drivers for money, how would you like to experience money in the future?

Explore the details of what it would be like if you were in a great space with money:
1. First, how would you feel? Write down every emotion you want to positively associate with money. Get every emotion down on paper and make a note of the 3 most important. Let's call this your money happy place.

2. Now we want to review all of the things you said about money and rephrase them in a way that is more supportive. For example, if one of your go to phrases is 'I can't afford it', rephrase by saying, 'I choose not to buy this right now', notice how that feels. Do this for every single phrase that came up, rephrase it in a light that is more supportive of you becoming unstuck and moving forward financially.

3. Ok now we want to identify how would this look, what would you be doing? Who would you be with? Where would you be?

So now that you have how you'd want to feel, hear and be, I want you to close your eyes, take a deep breath and visualize you in your happy money place. Take a deep breath in, and out, in and out.

Imagine yourself immersed in this vision, imagine feeling all those feelings you said were most important. Hear yourself saying all those reframed phrases….. Once you have this vision I want you to turn those feelings all the way up, double the intensity of those feelings, double it again, really imagine feeling great about money. Turn up the colors of this picture of your happy money place, the happy sounds….and when it can't get any more intense I want you to put your thumb and your index finger together and squeeze down as hard as you can…all the while turning up the intensity of all those emotions you captured above, all the ones you said were most important. When you're ready take another breath in, and open your eyes.

By doing this exercise what we have done is anchored in, a more positive emotional state for you and your relationship with money.

So I want to you to practice this visualization regularly and especially any time you feel anxious or worried about money or a money situation. Here's why:

Our subconscious mind literally doesn't know the difference between what's real and what isn't.

That's why you can have a dream about your partner cheating and spend the day feeling like you could literally kill him. I know you know what I'm talking about!!!

Because emotionally, you really went through that

Your unconscious mind really took you there. You felt every emotional aspect of that dream because it felt real and in your unconscious mind, it was real.

So by practicing this visualization as a regular habit, we are creating a new state of money mind and one that is supportive of our wildest financial dreams.

Remember my love; at the end of the day you were put on this earth to thrive not simply survive. Abundance is all around; you just have to create a new experience where you can truly see it.

Dominique Mullally is a Money & Mindset coach who empowers women in business how to step into their financial power, create strategies to increase their income and unapologetically create financial success.

Dominique uses her expertise in Financial Advising, NLP, EFT and Hypnotherapy to empower women with the knowledge of how to make personal and business money matters easy, rewarding and most of all FUN. She focuses on healing your relationship with money from the inside out, releasing the shame, fear, guilt or anxiety that may be attached to you and your money - allowing the real possibility to create real wealth.

FREE GIFT, Money Mantra Meditation:
https://dominiquemullally.lpages.co/money-mantra-meditation-dec-2018/

Follow Dominique on Instagram:
www.instagram.com/dominiquemullally

Join her FB group: www.facebook.com/groups/497678653747066/
Dominique's FB Page: www.facebook.com/dominiquemullally1/
Visit her website: www.dominiquemullally.com

STAY CONNECTED

to

'The Money Code & How To Crack It'

by liking the FaceBook Page:

https://www.facebook.com/moneycodebook/

STAY CONNECTED TO THE AUTHORS
Stephanie J. Alvarez - www.themoneyhealer.com

Tesa Colvin - www.facebook.com/BMyMBA

Sami Hageman - www.eatpraybudget.com

Gemma James - www.facebook.com/FreedomLifeCEO

Dominique Mullally - www.dominiquemullally.com

Marnita Oppermann - www.marnita.co.za

Nicole Redmond - http://www.redmondlegacycoaching.com/

Maria Kathlyn Tan – www.maria-miracles.com/

STAY CONNECTED TO THE FOREWORD AUTHOR
Auguste Crenshaw – www.augustecrenshaw.com

(A Division of Borrow My MBA, LLC)

Books that impact don't happen every day, but they should.

As thought leaders and service based business owners such as speakers, coaches, consultant, and the like, we are continuously working to improve the lives of others.

Our missions are personal, they are important; they are needed by so many to live their very best lives. So our messages cannot be taken lightly, and they must be shared so they can reach the people who need them the most.

If you're ready to write a book that impacts and starts a movement, lets connect and schedule some time to make it happen!
http://borrowmymba.com/work-with-me/

Printed in Great Britain
by Amazon

19353811R00061